AF270372

Geology Zone

Soils

by Julie Murray

Dash!
LEVELED READERS
An Imprint of Abdo Zoom • abdobooks.com

Level 1 – Beginning
Short and simple sentences with familiar words or patterns for children who are beginning to understand how letters and sounds go together.

Level 2 – Emerging
Longer words and sentences with more complex language patterns for readers who are practicing common words and letter sounds.

Level 3 – Transitional
More developed language and vocabulary for readers who are becoming more independent.

abdobooks.com

Published by Abdo Zoom, a division of ABDO, PO Box 398166, Minneapolis, Minnesota 55439. Copyright © 2025 by Abdo Consulting Group, Inc. International copyrights reserved in all countries. No part of this book may be reproduced in any form without written permission from the publisher. Dash!™ is a trademark and logo of Abdo Zoom.

Printed in the United States of America, North Mankato, Minnesota.
102024
012025

Photo Credits: Getty Images, Shutterstock
Production Contributors: Kenny Abdo, Jennie Forsberg, Grace Hansen, John Hansen
Design Contributors: Candice Keimig, Neil Klinepier

Library of Congress Control Number: 2024936544

Publisher's Cataloging in Publication Data

Names: Murray, Julie, author.
Title: Soils / by Julie Murray
Description: Minneapolis, Minnesota : Abdo Zoom, 2025 | Series: Geology zone | Includes online resources and index.
Identifiers: ISBN 9781098287207 (lib. bdg.) | ISBN 9781098287900 (ebook) | ISBN 9781098288259 (Read-to-me ebook)
Subjects: LCSH: Soils--Juvenile literature. | Earth (Soils)--Juvenile literature. | Rocks--Identification--Juvenile literature. | Geology--Juvenile literature. | Earth sciences--Juvenile literature. | Pedology (Soil science)--Juvenile literature.
Classification: DDC 577--dc23

Table of Contents

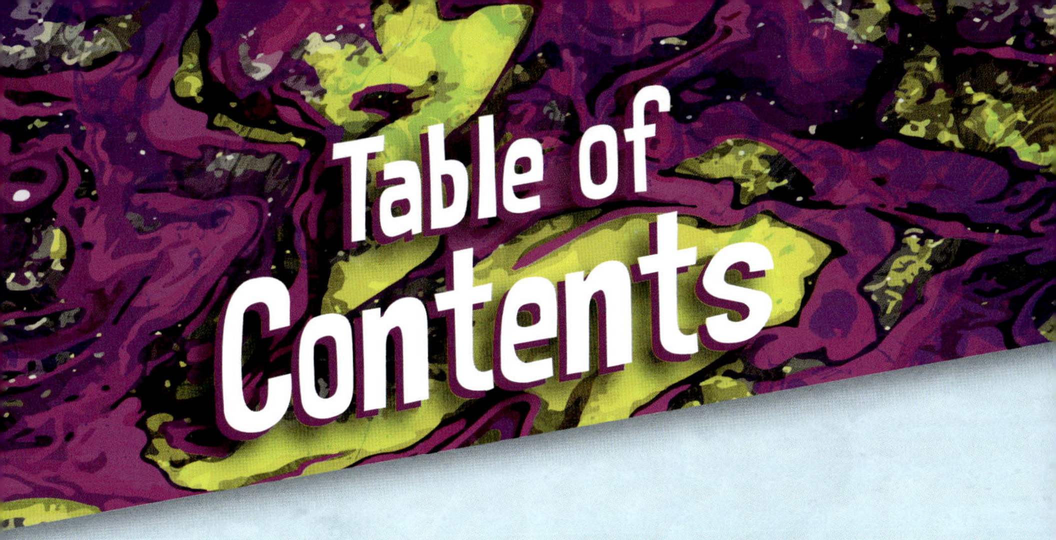

Soils

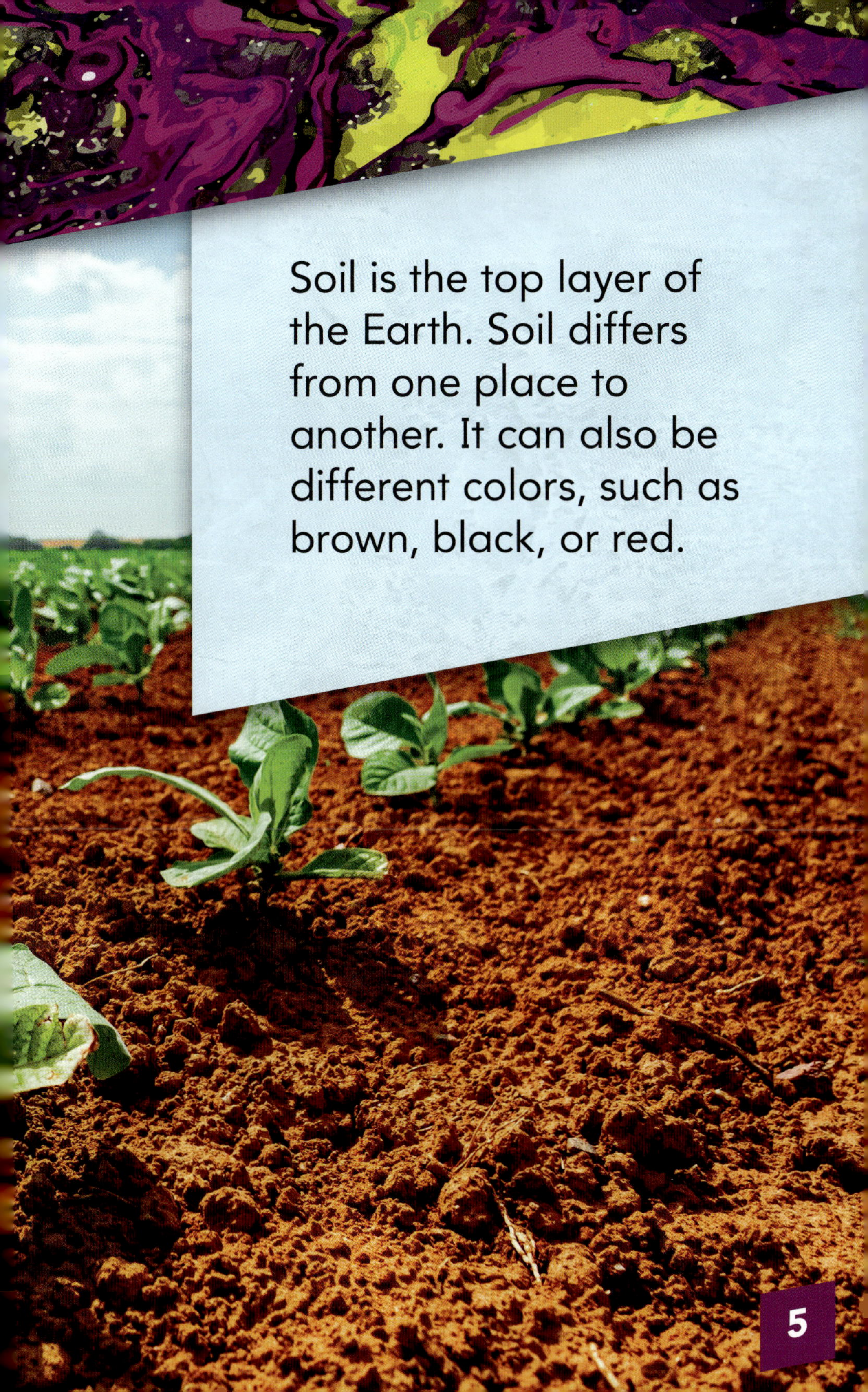

Soil is the top layer of the Earth. Soil differs from one place to another. It can also be different colors, such as brown, black, or red.

Soil Ingredients

Soil has four main ingredients. They are organic matter, **minerals**, water, and gas. Organic matter is a material made by living beings and the remains of living beings.

Soil is filled with tiny beings called microbes. Microbes break down organic matter and recycle **nutrients**. Bacteria and **fungi** are examples of these.

Earthworms play an important role in keeping soil healthy. They feed on organic materials. Their **nutrient**-rich waste mixes with the soil. Their tunnels allow water and air to move through the soil.

Soil contains different amounts of sand, **silt**, and clay. These **minerals** determine how soil acts and feels. Loam has an equal balance of these minerals. It is the best soil for growing plants.

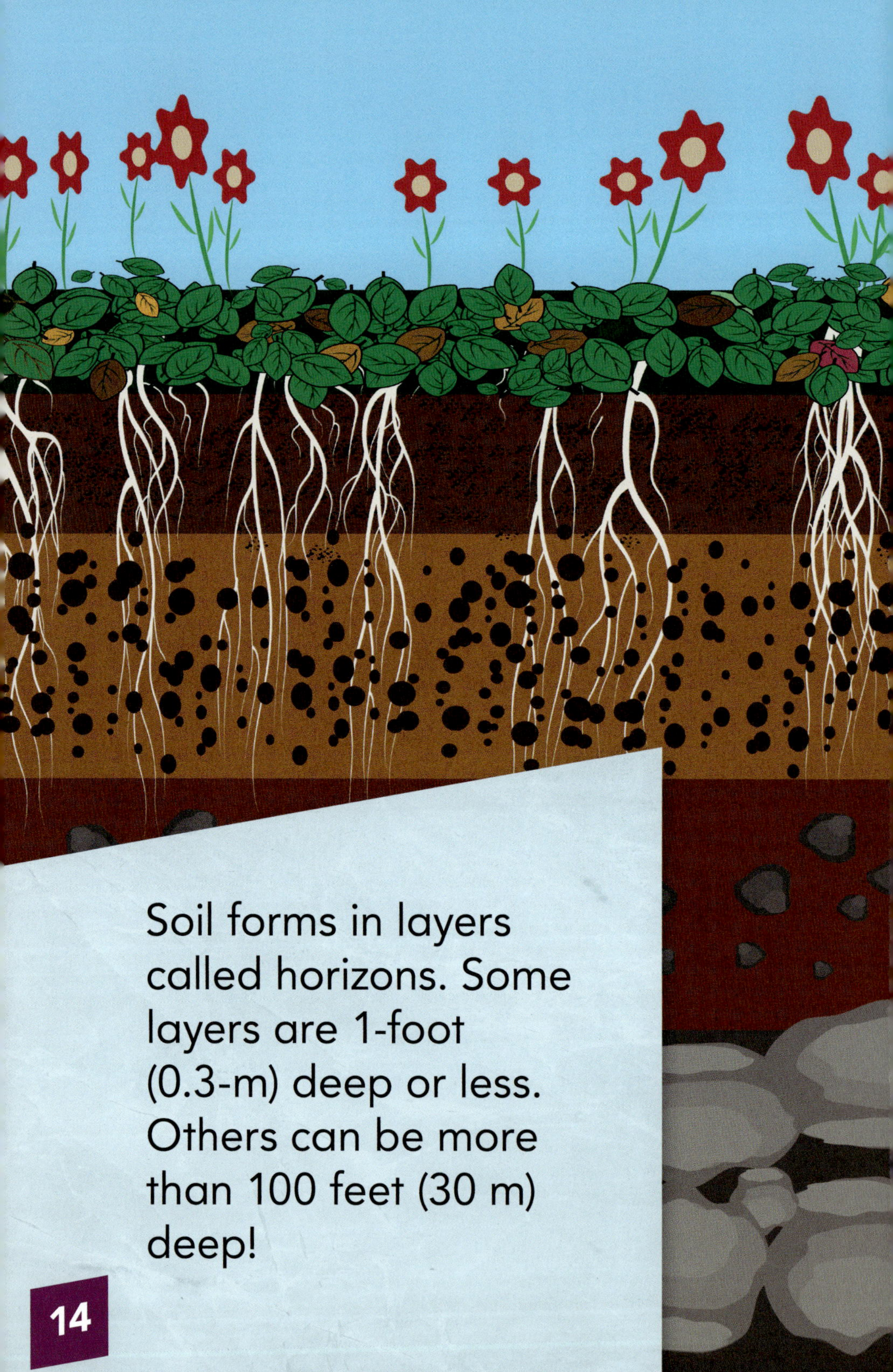

Soil forms in layers called horizons. Some layers are 1-foot (0.3-m) deep or less. Others can be more than 100 feet (30 m) deep!

Soil layers

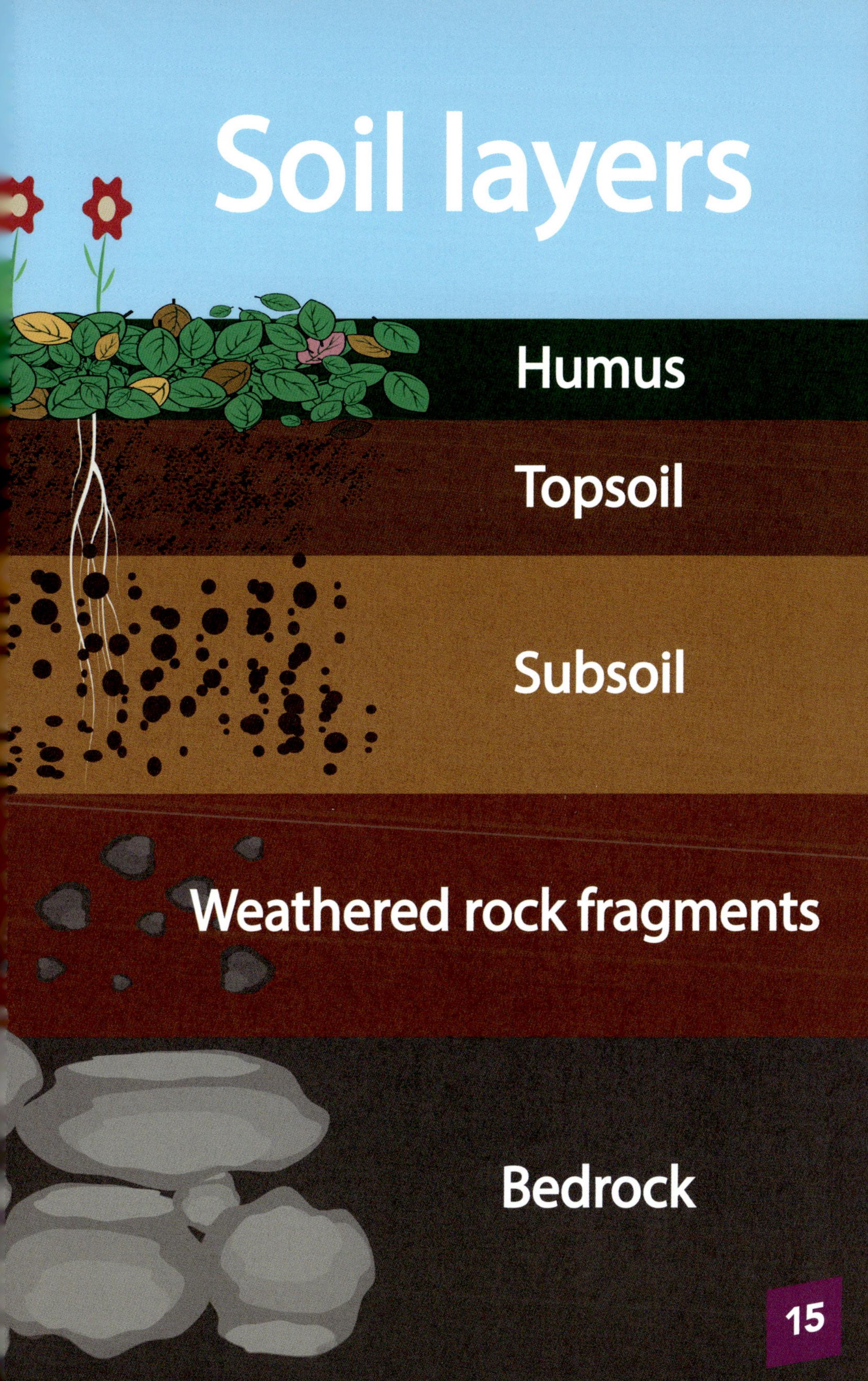

Erosion changes soil over time. Wind blows soil from one place to another. Water washes soil away with rain and mudslides. Glaciers move soil and erode the land.

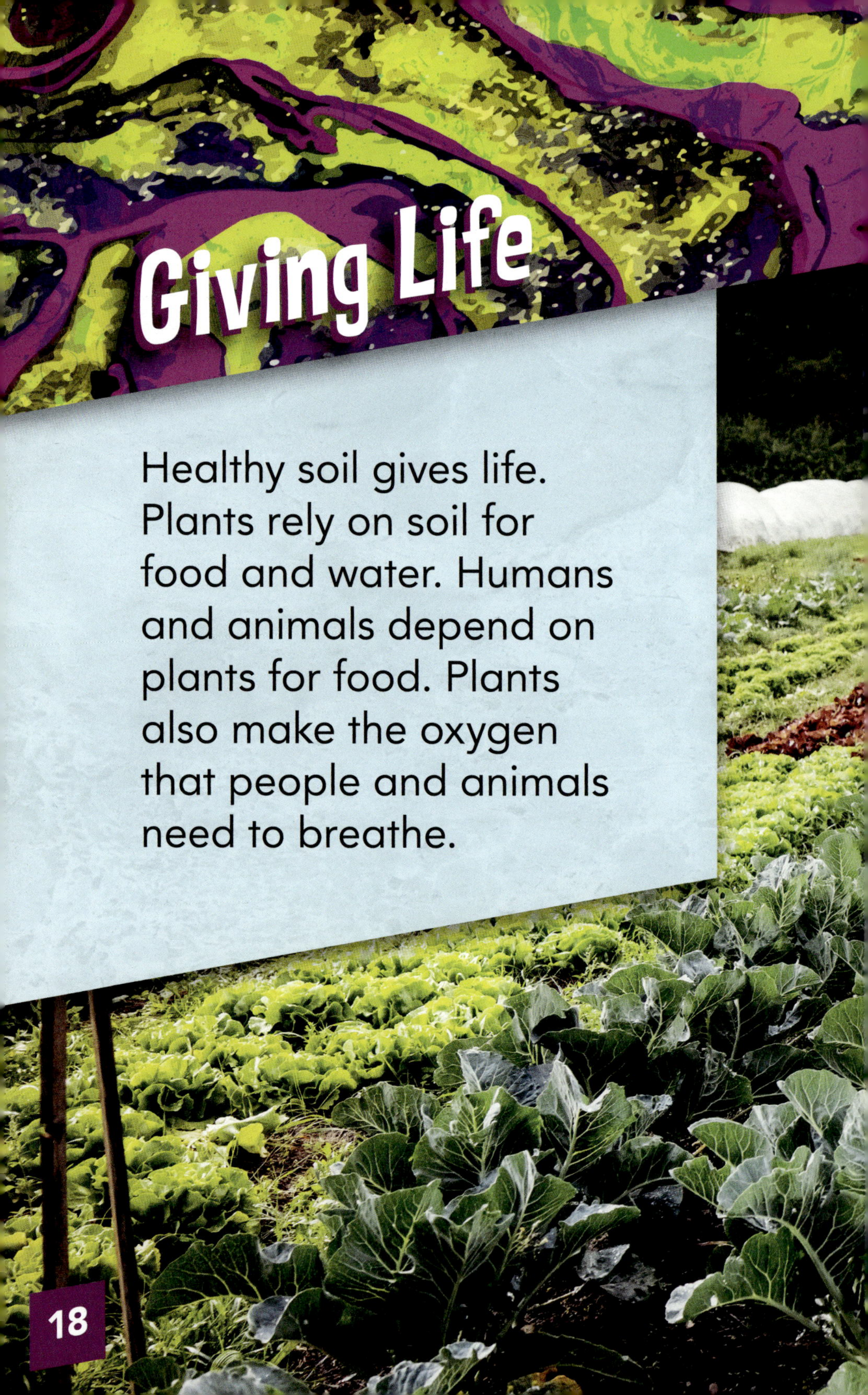

Giving Life

Healthy soil gives life. Plants rely on soil for food and water. Humans and animals depend on plants for food. Plants also make the oxygen that people and animals need to breathe.

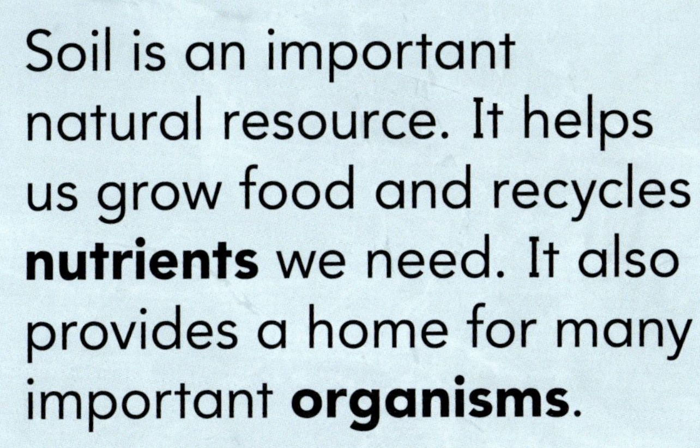

Soil is an important natural resource. It helps us grow food and recycles **nutrients** we need. It also provides a home for many important **organisms**.

- A scientist who studies soil is called a pedologist.

- Scientists have identified more than 20,000 different kinds of soil in the United States!

- Composting is a way to improve the quality of soil. It breaks down organic materials and adds **nutrients** to soil.

erosion – wearing away of the earth's surface by wind or water.

fungi – the plural of fungus, which is one of a large group of living things that appear similar to plants but cannot make their own food using sunlight in the way plants do.

mineral – a substance formed in the earth that is not of an animal or a plant.

nutrient – something in food that helps people, animals, and plants live and grow.

organism – an individual living thing, such as a plant or animal.

silt – fine particles of earth, clay, or sand that eventually settle out of water.

Index

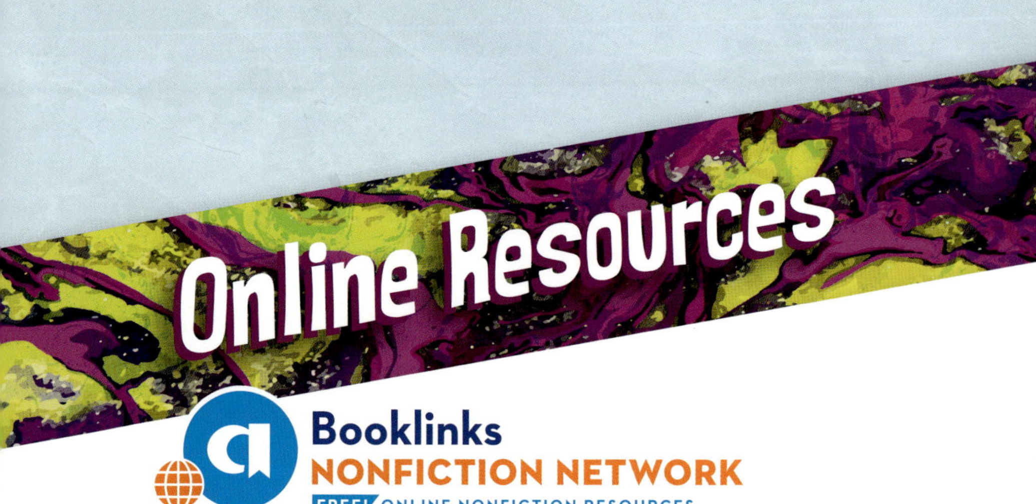

Online Resources

Booklinks
NONFICTION NETWORK
FREE! ONLINE NONFICTION RESOURCES

To learn more about soils, please visit **abdobooklinks.com** or scan this QR code. These links are routinely monitored and updated to provide the most current information available.